99¢

YOUR MEMORY—

SPEEDWAY TO SUCCESS

in Earning, Learning and Living

Your Memory--
Speedway to Success

in Earning, Learning and Living

FEATURING

The Auto-Magic* Memory Method

by O. W. "Bill" Hayes

An Exposition–Banner Book • *Illustrated*

EXPOSITION PRESS   NEW YORK

NOTE:
The Auto-Magic* Memory Method is the registered trade
name for the memory system devised and taught by
the author.

Published, October, 1958
Second Printing, April, 1959
Third Printing, May, 1959
Fourth Printing, December, 1959
Fifth Printing, November, 1960
Sixth Printing, December, 1964
Seventh Printing, January, 1965

EXPOSITION PRESS INC., 386 Fourth Avenue, New York 16, N.Y.

THIRD EDITION

PRINTED IN THE UNITED STATES OF AMERICA
BY GANIS AND HARRIS, NEW YORK

Dedicated to

the hostesses of

Braniff International Airways

ACKNOWLEDGMENTS

For their encouragement and assistance, the author wishes to express his grateful appreciation to Dr. G. V. Brindley, Jr., Letha Easterwood, Jean Sparks, G. V. Phillips Sr., Paul Boyd, and R. E. Richardson, and to the late Ed Yarbrough, as well as all the members of my family.

PREFACE

THIS PRIMER ON MEMORY TRAINING, though primarily for adults, is also suited for teachers and parents concerned with child education and development. It is in the early years of school attendance that boys and girls start out on the road to success. All educators agree that this road can be traveled more smoothly with the aid of a good memory.

A highly developed memory is one of a child's chief assets. It brings him high marks in school and gives him confidence, determination and poise: the keys to personal and social success. Most of all, it gives children an ability which will set the groundwork for their future success in the business or professional worlds.

This book is short. Its principles are direct and uncomplicated. The Auto-Magic* Memory Method makes learning to remember fun.

Parents and teachers will want to bring this book to the attention of their children and their pupils. They will want them to master the Auto-Magic* method.

This is not a hard job. Parents can work with their chil-

9

dren at home on week ends and evenings. Teachers can introduce the Auto-Magic* system in the classroom and teach their pupils to use it in the course of a few hours.

The teacher can read this book and master its principles in one evening at home. She can then present these to her pupils on the following day and review them in detail during the rest of the week, teaching the children how to apply the Auto-Magic* system to all of their courses.

Within that week parents and teachers will note a marked improvement in the ability of the children to remember names, dates, places, arithmetic tables and formulas.

And the children, noticing this added ability in themselves with the joy that all children feel in being able to do something more than usual, will become more eager and attentive pupils, and will be more solidly assured of the success they choose for themselves.

O. W. H.

CONTENTS

....

INTRODUCTION

IT IS THE INTENTION of the author of this book to prepare a condensed memory course that will implant itself indelibly on the minds of its readers. Many memory courses have been published that are not simplified in any form and, therefore, scare the reader before he ever gets started. The following presentation is designed to give a boost to the memory power of people in all walks of life and all ages. Intense desire on the part of the reader, coupled with attention and repetition, will solidify that person's memory.

It is suggested that some of these exercises and lessons be discussed with friends and other members of the family. This will help to make a game of improving your memory and will rub off on those with whom you come in contact. The brevity of the book will, I am sure, have tremendous appeal for you, because in one short evening's time and with a little bit of practice you can become a person with an enviable memory. Good luck! I know you can do it!

YOUR MEMORY—

SPEEDWAY TO SUCCESS

in Earning, Learning and Living

SECTION ONE

MEMORY MAGIC

IT'S EASY TO REMEMBER

....

To Prove a Point

A DAY NEVER PASSES that someone of you does not say, "I have the worst memory in the world." If you really feel this deficiency, with a little effort you can do something about it. I propose to show you how.

This chapter is *not* directed toward assisting you to memorize more easily. It is designed to prove a point.

Example: When arising in the morning, you realize that certain errands must be accomplished before nightfall. These may include:

> Purchasing a pound of bacon,
> a package of tape,
> a box of matches,
> a bouquet of flowers,
> a bottle of ink,
> a flashlight,
> a jar of mustard,
> a mousetrap;
> Getting your glasses adjusted,
> Paying the telephone bill.

19

Now that you have read these items, see how many you can remember without looking back. Write the errands down, if you wish. The average person remembers six or seven. If you did not recall all ten, then you probably desire to proceed to learn the Auto-Magic* method.

This time re-read the list, but do it in the following manner. Group the items as you come to them. Visualize a pound package of sliced bacon with lighted matches standing between the slices. The entire package is held together by a large adhesive tape. This looks rather strange, but in the strangeness of it lies an important clue toward the ability to recall at once almost anything that you care to remember.

Next, visualize a beautiful bouquet of flowers standing alongside the previous package. Standing by the flowers is a good friend holding a flashlight over the flowers. As the person tilts the light an amazing thing happens: jet black ink comes from the flashlight and pours all over the lovely bouquet. Some of the ink spatters on the bacon. Now, you have two groups of items. Let us add a third.

As you are wondering how to clean up the mess you hear a loud snap and, glancing around, you see a mousetrap closed over your eyeglasses. It has broken a lens. The lens has been smeared with mustard. Just as you are reaching for the mousetrap, you hear a tinkling sound and are startled to find coins falling out of your telephone.

Now the articles are grouped by three's, with the additional odd item of the telephone rounding out the things that you are trying to remember. Turn away from the page and see how many items you can recall. You should remember ten. If you do, then I have "proved a point."

THE AUTO-MAGIC*
MEMORY METHOD

To MAKE MEMORY TRAINING a simple maneuver for any active mind, I heartily recommend the Auto-Magic* system. It is simple, yet tremendously effective.

Example: Visualize each of the following parts of an automobile.

1 Radiator ornament
2 Headlights
3 Front bumper guards
4 Wheels (preferably front)
5 Door handle (preferably front)
6 Window (preferably front)
7 Horn button
8 Steering wheel
9 Windshield wipers (working fine)
10 Hand brake
11 Speedometer
12 Dashboard clock
13 Glove compartment
14 Front seat (beside You)

23

15　Ash tray (side of Rear Seat)
16　Back seat
17　Trunk compartment
18　Taillights
19　Rear license plate
20　Objects behind you (whatever you see in the mirror)

Now read the list over. Visualize it as you read it.

There are reasons for taking the items in the suggested order. For example: there is *one* radiator cap. Whatever the first thing is that you desire to remember, place it on this object. If you are in need of a loaf of bread, for instance, picture it impaled or tied on the radiator cap. If you want to remember to buy catsup, then picture a huge bottle as the

radiator ornament itself and stick a big catsup label on the bottle. See this in your "magic eye." Number two is so designated because there are usually two headlights; number three, because of three bumper guards; number four, for the four wheels of every car. Because of the procedure we are to follow, however, it would be easier to tie the object we wish to remember to the front wheel.

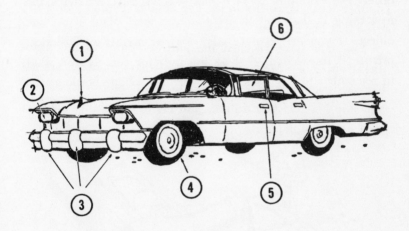

Number five is the next part in order. There are five handles (if you include the trunk handle), so place the thing to be memorized on the front door handle. Number six is the window above it. Most cars have six windows. Number seven can be placed firmly in your mind if you will follow this advice: Seven is the horn button. Blow the horn.

"Gabriel's horn is heard in Heaven—that's why ours is number seven." Pause here and reflect on what you have read. Repeat them. Make sure that you can remember all of them.

Proceed to number eight. This is the steering wheel. "Turn the wheel before it's too late; that's why we call it number eight." For number nine remember: "Windshield wipers are working fine; that's why they are number nine." Number ten: "Grab the brake for number ten, so you won't strike that big fat hen."

You now have reached the halfway point in the Auto-Magic* Memory Method. If you feel that ten items are all that you ever will wish or need to recall at one time, you may stop here. If you do not, join me in discussing the next parts of the automobile.

Number eleven: "Speedometer is always eleven; drive too fast, maybe Heaven" Twelve: The clock is twelve. Always picture it set at twelve o'clock.

Thirteen requires extra imagination. The glove compartment is opened and in it there is a black cat with a big number 13 painted on its side. This is number thirteen.

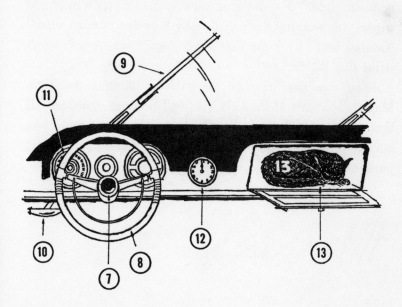

Fourteen is the front seat beside you. This comes from picturing your sweetheart sitting beside you. The fourteenth of February is Valentine's Day. Picture mentally the rear-seat ash tray as number fifteen. Have fifteen cigarette butts

crowded into the ash tray. Sixteen: This is the back seat itself. Seated on it is a very pretty girl, your sweetheart's sister, who is "Sweet Sixteen."

Seventeen is the inside of the back, or the trunk compartment. Picture seven teenage friends who have sneaked into the trunk for a free ride.

Eighteen signifies the red stoplights. You stop being a girl and become a lady when you are eighteen. See large red stoplights. Nineteen is next. It is the rear license plate. Tie the object to it. Most license plates have the number 19 on them. The last of the numbers is twenty. See it in the rearview mirror. It is following you down the road. What you see is number twenty.

This completes the Auto-Magic* Twenty. Re-read the list and the instructions. Picture each as you do so. Now, try to remember five, then ten, then fifteen, then twenty miscellaneous articles. Use them in conjunction with the Auto-Magic* system.

It is essential that you repeat the Auto-Magic* system over and over until each part of the automobile comes to mind as soon as the number is called. A good practice drill is to jumble a series of numbers from one to twenty then see how fast you can fill in the blanks. Try it.

Seven———	Twelve———
Six———	Nine———
Nineteen———	Thirteen———
Eight———	Five———
Four———	Eighteen———
One———	Three———
Seventeen———	Sixteen———
Fifteen———	Fourteen———
Twenty———	Eleven———
Two———	Ten———

Try this several times.

Now, go over the list of parts of the automobile. Place the correct number after each part.

Rear license plate——	Headlights——
Back seat——	Front door handle——
Front seat——	Horn button——
Glove compartment——	Rear ash tray——
Radiator ornament——	Speedometer——
Front wheel——	Bumper guards——
Windshield wiper——	Mirror——
Hand brake——	Steering wheel——
Taillights——	Dashboard clock——
Trunk compartment——	Window (left front)——

Rearrange these parts on a separate sheet of paper and see how fast and how accurately you can fill them in correctly. Do this at least once every day until you can do it with perfection in 45 seconds or less.

Repeating anything that you wish to remember is of utmost importance. Desire, repetition, and retention come in that order as a code to success in memory training.

To Clean the Slate

In order to wipe the slate clean, after completing your project, always see *that part* of the automobile alone again. In other words, let us suppose that you are going to the store to buy bread, cheese, and sardines. Picture the bread on the #1 (radiator cap), the cheese smeared on the #2 (head-lights) and the sardines tied by their tails to the #3 (bumper). After you have purchased these items, then see the auto parts clean of all these objects, and you are ready to start again.

Suggestions to Follow

Every time you see your automobile or picture an automobile in your magic eye, see the radiator ornament first. If you have placed an object or errand on the radiator ornament, then this object will immediately come to mind.

Make lists of twenty miscellaneous objects or errands and practice regularly to see how much your memory is improving, or take a newspaper or magazine and try this exercise. It will prove to be fun and you will startle your friends with your ability. Look at page one of a magazine or newspaper and select a major item or advertisement on this page. Mentally place it on # 1 (radiator ornament). Next turn to page two and do the same thing to #2 (the headlights). Continue through the first twenty pages.

You will find that with very little practice you will retain information accurately and with amazing speed.

Examples:

Page one has a story about a new weapon the nation's scientists have devised. Picture this weapon on top of or striking your radiator ornament.

Page two has an advertisement about daily specials at a downtown market. Picture a basket of groceries placed over each of the front headlights.

Page three contains a story about a new ape that has been brought to this country for one of the zoos. See this ape with your magic eye. Visualize him sitting on the front bumper guards. Continue in this manner, and soon you will find that the retention of all desired objects and items becomes easier.

Study a group of items in a display case for a while. Turn away and name as many of the items as you can.

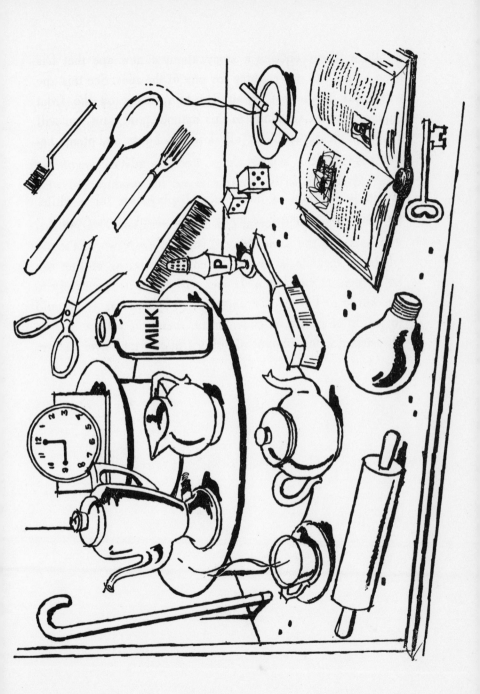

How to Absorb

In reading a book, letter, article, or whatever it may be, picture each scene or action as you read. Pick up a newspaper or a magazine and read a few sentences. Picture as you read. Do this several times. Read an advertisement. See how clearly the writer has portrayed his product and what it will do.

With the next sermon, speech, or even conversation that you hear, do the same thing. Listen to every word. Picture what the speaker is saying. A condensation or outline can be written as you listen. If you will listen as attentively to the words of the teacher, lecturer, or speaker as you would to words of praise or endearment, then you will be sure to absorb a greater amount of subject matter than ever before.

Exaggeration and Amplification

Exaggeration and amplification can improve anyone's memory. If an object is normally large, make it either larger or a great deal smaller. Do this even to the point of making the object seem ridiculous. It will stay with you a great deal more easily and also longer. If you hear a name, or someone tells you something that you desire to remember, amplify the sound or possible effect of it. This is more effective in single instances than in group effort. In other words, if Mr. Hansen tells you that his name is Hansen, then picture this man shouting his name or whispering it to you. Anything other than the normal is easier to recall.

Outlines

Initialing and indexing may well serve as a ready reference outline for public speakers and for students in classroom recitations.

Example: In delivering a talk on salesmanship, a speaker may desire to include the following good points; Fairness to competition, Intelligence, Gratitude, Honor, Truth. These, when initialed, spell FIGHT. As the speaker completes the discussion of one point and is ready to bring out the next point, he need only reach for the next letter in the word FIGHT, or whatever initialed word or code he has chosen. You may want to tie these points or code words into the Auto-Magic* system. Place the first code word (FIGHT in this case; picture fighters) on your radiator ornament, the second code word on the headlights, and so on. This will serve as double insurance for bringing these code words readily to mind.

Geographical Gems

The three Pacific coast states are Washington, Oregon, and California. *WOC* or *COW*. See a cow lying, sunning herself, on the seaside of the Pacific Ocean. Picture this in your magic eye. *COW* represents the initials of the Pacific Coast states.

You can

Another example: There is only one place in the United States where four states join. In order to remember the four states, just think of the word *UCAN*. You can remember the four states, Utah, Colorado, Arizona, and New Mexico by these initials.

Still another example: The five Great Lakes can be pictured as flooding the country side with *HOMES* floating on them. See these *HOMES* in your magic eye. *H* is for Huron, *O* for Ontario, *M* for Michigan, *E* for Erie, and *S* for Superior. This will stay with you.

More Geography

Many persons have trouble recalling which of two cities, Bismarck and Pierre, is the capital of North Dakota and which is the capital of South Dakota. *B* is before *P* in the alphabet. *B*, therefore, comes first. It is on the top. The top state is the northernmost state; therefore, Bismarck is the capital of North Dakota.

Lincoln is the capital of Nebraska, yet, Omaha is the state's largest city. Write out the word *Lincoln* and then draw a large *O* around it. These exercises and examples can pertain to any subject during school years or afterward. Historical figures, lines of succession, battles, military leaders, a multitude of subjects can be eased into the Auto-Magic* and associated methods of memory improvement.

For purposes of memorizing the presidents of the United States, the Auto-Magic* system is ideal. Going through the automobile twice to fit in the necessary numbers suitably or merely picturing the presidents and tying them into a story or initialing system as you go, you can easily recall the names. George Washington, being the first president, could be depicted as a washing machine or the Washington Monument on the radiator ornament of the car. For John Adams, the second president, you could have a dam with water flowing out of each headlight of the car. Mutt and Jeff could be pictured on the bumper of the car, fighting with each other. This would depict Jefferson. You could have a boxing ring in Madison Square Garden on the front tire of the car for President Madison. For the fifth president you could have the Monroe Doctrine wrapped around the door handle and tied with a pretty ribbon; and so on through all the presidents. If you wish to fit them into a story, you can do so with the greatest of ease.

Foreign Languages

The study of foreign languages can be made a great deal easier by following the advice of Socrates, who said, "Never use a word without seeing in nature that for which the word stands." A mental picture of the word based upon real live things, with the use of association as a crutch can be of tremendous assistance to the language student.

In French, for instance,

bleu means blue
couleur means color
jaune means yellow (as in jaundice)
rouge means red
père means father
maison means house.

In Latin *aqua* means water (from which comes the word *aquatic)*
cogitare means to think (or to cogitate)
pater means father
arbor means tree
femina means woman
frater means brother.

In Spanish *jaula* is jail or cage
frio means frigid or cold
alto means high
diablo means devil
toro means bull

Rhymes and Codes

We are all familiar with the rhyme "Thirty days hath September . . ." Many times in childhood we turned to it for the information that it contains. Some older persons still refer to it as a simple and sound method for ascertaining the number of days in a stated month.

Codes that we develop ourselves are very effective. Those that we prepare, to include certain information, can be a sure-fire way to success in memorizing. Use of initials can be helpful also.

Example: You wish to learn the capitals of the six New England states: Boston, Concord, Hartford, Augusta, Montpelier, and Providence. Think of the word *B–champ*. To help it make sense, say to yourself, "Boston is the largest, so B is the champ." Immediately, *B* for Boston, *C* for Concord, *H* for Hartford, and so forth, will come to mind.

After speaking before a convention of educators at Kingsville, Texas, in 1958, I talked with a number of the audience following the program. One very experienced lady said that she had been able to recall how to spell the word *geography* when she was a child by the use of a little sentence that she had prepared and it had stayed with her over the years. She had the initialing system. This sentence was, "George Edward's old grandmother rode a pig home yesterday." This certainly was a vivid description, and you can see that it had lasting value.

Memory for Medics

The twelve cranial nerves are among the many things that must be memorized by all medical students. These twelve cranial nerves: olfactory, optic, oculomotor, trochlear, trigeminal, abducens, facial, auditory, glossopharyngeal, vagus, spinal accessory, and hypoglossal can be pictured easily with the Auto-Magic* system. The first, the olfactory, could be an old factory placed on the radiator ornament of the car; as number two, the optic nerve, could be placed with an eye seeing out of each of the automobile headlights. Some syllable or an exaggerated pronunciation of each of these words could be fitted into the entire Auto-Magic* picture, as in number six, *abducens*. You could picture someone being abducted and being caught as the window is jammed up to hold him.

Number seven, the facial, could be a face on the horn button; number eight, the steering wheel, could be two big ears to remind you that *auditory* is the word for the eighth cranial nerve. Number twelve, the hypoglossal, could be shown as a glossy shining hypodermic needle set in place as each hand of the clock, which is number twelve in the Auto-Magic* system. By stretching the imagination and making it work actively, you can bring to mind these medical terms.

Initialing these nerves to form a word or a sentence is another system that can work into a permanent memory rhyme. The one most used in medical schools throughout America is: "On old Olympus' towering top a Finn and German viewed a hof."

The bones of the wrist can be memorized easily by the initialing method or by the Auto-Magic* system. The Auto-Magic* system, through exaggerated pronunciations of words, is most effective. For instance, the scaphoid bone can be converted into a scaffold and placed as number one on the radiator ornament of the car, and so on through the bones of the wrist.

The muscles of the leg or any other series of parts or objects may be similarly placed.

Legal Assistance

The value of the Auto-Magic* method in simplifying memorization of legal terms is exemplified by its use in relation to the amendments to the Constitution. For instance, in order to memorize these most easily, you could picture them in place on the Auto-Magic* automobile; number one, dealing with freedom of religion, speech, press, assembly, and petition, could be pictured as a big Liberty Bell, or a Bible, printing press, or one of the objects or group of objects, placed upon the radiator ornament of the car. For the Second Amendment, the right to bear arms, you could have two bare arms hanging out of the two headlights. For number three, which pertains to the housing of soldiers, several soldiers in little toy houses could be placed along the bumper of the car.

Amendment number four, dealing with unlawful search and seizure, could be pictured as someone seizing the tire from your car and carrying it stealthily away, meanwhile holding a searchlight. For Amendment number five, double jeopardy, you could have two door handles or double door handles with a witness sitting on one and yourself sitting on the other with reference to the phrase that deals with not bearing witness against yourself. For Amendment number six, you could have the automobile window being wound up rapidly with reference to the "speedy trial by jury" and have the jurors sitting inside the window casing. Number seven, the trial by jury, could be shown by having the horn blown to assemble the jurors or the veniremen to sit around the horn button.

Number eight, in reference to excessive bail, could be pictured as rowboats around the steering wheel with someone bailing water out. For number nine, you might have two windshield wipers on the righthand side of the windshield, instead of one in front of you, to exemplify the phrase . . . "all rights not otherwise listed"; and so on through the twenty-two amendments, each of them being pictured and placed on an object of the car.

The Twenty-first Amendment, dealing with the repeal of the Eighteenth Amendment, being more than the twenty in the Auto-Magic* system, could be placed alongside the Eighteenth Amendment on one of the two taillights of the car. The Twenty-second Amendment, dealing with two terms for presidents, could be placed farther back down the highway, behind the Twentieth Amendment, as seen in the mirror on the car. These can be memorized permanently or on a temporary basis, as is true in any use of the Auto-Magic* system.

Salesmen's Samples

Nearly all salesmen necessarily carry catalogs. If they will develop the catalog by sections and tie it into the Auto-Magic* system as follows, I believe they will find it a great deal easier to locate items they wish to present to the customer as soon as he makes an inquiry.

If a salesman is selling pencil sharpeners and staplers, for instance, and they are in the first section of the catalog, he should place the first section mentally on the radiator ornament of his car. Section two of his catalog might deal with paper and paper supplies, carbon paper, duplicating machines and duplicator products. These can be grouped and visualized as the automobile headlights in the Auto-Magic* system and so on throughout the catalog.

The initialing system for salesmen is also of value. There is nothing that distresses a customer more than to have to wait while the salesman looks through his catalog to locate an item that he should have been able to turn to with the greatest of ease.

Appointments can be remembered very easily through the use of the Auto-Magic* system. If you had to see Mr. Lodge at 5 o'clock, you might picture the automobile door handle, which is Item No. 5, with a hunting lodge set there in place of the handle, then, in reviewing, you would know that it was Mr. Lodge with whom you had an appointment.

The proper pronunciation and repeated use of a customer's name is always most pleasing to him. It is highly recommended that all salesmen absorb and practice the section in this book on name retention.

School Days

The requirement of memorizing in the classroom varies with state educational policies. It also appears to go in cycles. The memorizing of poetry, parts in plays, symbols in chemistry, is an important part of the development of a youthful mind. If memory work in education can be made easier, or if retention can be improved or developed, then another of our goals has been achieved. A classroom instructor would feel a greater sense of accomplishment if, at the end of a lecture, the students had retained all or nearly all of the subject matter.

The fact that we can read a book or a newspaper is indication enough that all of us have good memories. If we did not, it would be impossible to remember hundreds and thousands of words that enable us to understand what we read.

To guide restive minds is our challenge. We may seem to use unusual methods, but, nonetheless, we find them effective.

AND SO HARD TO FORGET

PROBABLY THE KEY to all memory improvement can be termed organization–observation–attention–absorption–retention–recall. Using the first letter of each of these words, you get oo–aa–rr, which is fairly easy to remember. I say *organization*, because your thoughts must be organized. This can be done through the Auto-Magic* system. I use *observation*, because you must observe thoroughly what you read and what you see in order to recall it over the years; *attention*, because attention improves concentration, and concentration is the red carpet to both memorization and success. I say *absorption*, because through attention and concentration you are able to absorb the things that you observe and the thoughts and sights you have organized in your mind. *Retention* and *recall* come as a result of the first four. You can retain permanently and recall automatically through the Auto-Magic* method.

55

Organization

By organizing our thoughts and grouping them through the use of the Auto-Magic* system, you are able to reach into a mental file and pull out necessary information upon a moment's notice.

Observation

Practice observing the people that you meet, the things that you see, and the places where you go. Ask yourself questions about the things that you have seen and done during the day. Give yourself an extensive test. Try to sit in your living room and see every item in the kitchen and the color of each item. Ask yourself questions about the dashboard of your automobile and the location of the various gauges on it. Question yourself regarding the design and pattern in clothes that others have worn or the things in your own closet. This teaches you to observe more carefully.

Attention

Attention is the key to concentration. You can concentrate wherever your heart is. As long as you are not preoccupied, you have the power to retain and recall anything you have the desire to remember. If you desire to remember, you pay attention and therefore are able to memorize.

Absorption

Concentration and attention combine to permit our minds to absorb whatever we may see and whatever we may hear. Retention and recall are coupled because they work together. A great deal of satisfaction will be derived from attention to details. Your knowledge, personality, and income will greatly benefit from the improvement of your memory.

Spelling

The use of organization and retention in spelling is of the utmost value. If the speller will exaggerate the letter in the word that is normally left out, it will stay in his magic eye a great deal longer, probably on a permanent basis.

Examples: In regard to my own last name, it is often confused because the writer will leave out the letter *e*; therefore, I would suggest that you picture the name as follows: *hayEs*.

There are many other words that can be used in this same manner. The word *gauge* is often misspelled. In order to remember that the *u* belongs in the middle, you might mentally place yourself in the middle of a narrow-gauge track and see the train coming at you. You are in the middle: *gaUge*.

The word license is another one that can easily be misspelled. To remember to put the *s* in license, a person could write it out and put the dollar mark instead of the *s* because a license costs money: *licen$e*.

If you wish to omit a letter, such as in spelling the word *sheriff*, pretty often the speller will put two *r*'s and two *f*'s in it or become confused as to where the *r*'s and *f*'s belong. I would suggest that you amplify the large *R* as follows: *sheRiff*. Also, it can be done by misspelling the word as follows: *sherriff, she riff*. Draw a slash mark or an *x* through the letter; then erase it, then write it again, drawing the line through it: *sherfiff*. You will further implant on your mind that the extra *r* does not belong in the word. This can be done with an innumerable list of words and will permanently remain in your mind attempting to spell it.

In spelling *knowledge* the letter *d* is often left out; therefore, write it in the following manner: *knowleDge*. You might even circle the capitalized letter, which would be of value in remembering the spelling. By repeating these various exercises and thinking up a few of your own, I believe your spelling difficulties will be greatly reduced.

SECTION TWO

YOU SEE A FACE BEFORE YOU

The sweetest sound . . . the sweetest sound of all . . .
is the sound of your own name. Everyone likes to hear his
own name. Everyone resents being called by a wrong or
mispronounced name.

Before World War II, I was asked to speak before a
civic organization in Nashua, New Hampshire. While waiting for the dinner to begin, I was introduced to over fifty
strangers. Later, while we were seated at the table, waiting
for dessert, the master of ceremonies discovered that I could
recall the name of everyone I had met. Accordingly, he
suggested to me that, when I acknowledged my introduction, I should greet everyone in the audience by name. I
doubted the value of this and questioned the reasoning behind it, but I agreed to try it. Frankly, it astonished and
pleased the entire group. I have been doing this effectively
ever since.

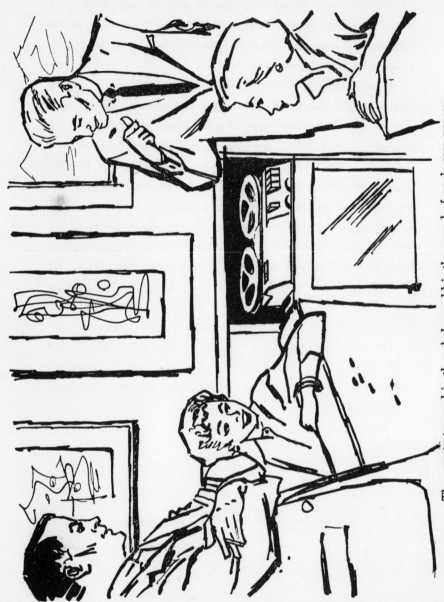

The sweetest sound in the whole world is the sound of one's own name.

On over five hundred occasions and to audiences totalling over 25,000 people, I have used this response to an introduction. To date, I have missed five names at such events. My greatest accomplishment was before several hundred surprised members of the Washington, D.C., Rotary Club in October, 1956. On one occasion, before the Exchange Club in Saint Catherine's, Ontario, my audience apparently had been tipped off to my "surprise" procedure, for upon arising, I found the entire membership moving around the room, exchanging seats. This presented an additional challenge that I successfully met.

As instructor of "The Technique of Memorization" course at the Texas State Police Academy I was able to address each student by his proper name by the end of the first one-hour class. I use this same procedure in my work as a guest lecturer at the hostess training school of a major airline.

My fabulous memory for names has given me added prestige, personality, and income. By following instructions, you too, can become most adept at this necessary part of anyone's education.

If one really *wants* to remember a name, he can do so much more easily than if he has no incentive. Intense desire is the number one requisite for the retention of a name. The example that I like best is to use this: "You see a beautiful girl (or an attractive man), and the name stays with you." This is true, of course, because you really desire to remember it.

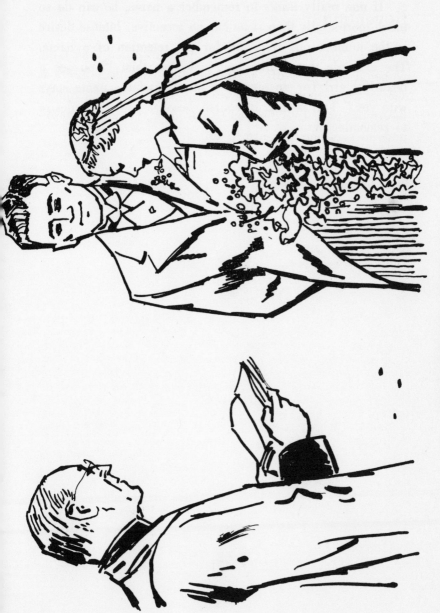

Attention Is Where the Heart Lies

Repetition

When you meet someone for the first time, repeat the name at the time of the introduction and then insert it several times into the general conversation. If the opportunity presents itself for you to introduce the new acquaintance to someone, be sure to use it.

Repeat the name; if necessary, ask how to spell it. . . .
Use it in conversation and upon departure. . . .
Associate it with someone or something. . . .
Note and exaggerate the most notable features. . . .
Later, write the name and read it aloud. . . .
Preferably, use last name only. . . .
Some time after meeting the person, test your memory
of the name. . . .
Relate the person to others of the same last name. . . .

Last Name Only

One of the most common mistakes is the attempt to learn both first and last names. Always—I repeat, always—pay attention to the *last* name only. A person never can be offended if called by his last name with Mr., Mrs., or Miss properly affixed. The first name can come later, and usually is given by the person himself. It is easier to have only one name to remember, and the fact that last names are generally much more distinctive makes your improvement in recalling names fall into line twice as fast.

If, sometime, you find yourself unable to recall a name, run through the alphabet letter by letter, and the name will come through.

CARICATURING

....

ONE OF THE GREATEST GUIDES to name retention is the singling out of one feature in a face. This can be amplified by the use of the caricaturing system. When you see a caricature in a newspaper or magazine, you find that the person has been caricatured by the amplification of the outstanding feature of his or her face. This method is highly recommended for the memorizing of names and faces on a permanent basis. This is one of the *most important features* in this *entire* publication.

You meet Mr. Jones. He has average features. You cannot find anything unusual about Mr. Jones. You could take the last four letters of his name, however, and scramble them to spell nose . . . n-o-s-e, and then see Mr. Jones pulled along by a J-shaped hook in his nose. The picture, so ridiculous and yet so vivid, will stay with you.

Many have told me at the outset that they might make an embarrassing mistake by calling a person by the wrong name. In the Jones case, they might say Mr. Hook. Repetition of this system, however, will establish confidence, and eventually security in the knowledge that you are right.

Here are some further examples to use as a test. How would you associate the names of Garfield, Simon, Butterson, Carmichael, Bussell, Finch, Culpepper, Ramsey, Yankowski and Selman? Try it yourself before you read my suggestions. No doubt there will be various suggestions. There can be many pictures for each name.

I would see a big fish (a gar) in a field . . . Mr. Garfield. I would picture Mr. Simon as sighing and moaning on alternate breaths. Mr. Butterson would be spreading butter on a big, red setting sun. Mr. Carmichael would be driving a car shaped like a microphone (or with a "mike" on the radiator cap) into the gates of hell.

Mr. Bussell could be selling a bus . . . the bus with a big number one on it, meaning that the bus comes first . . .

before the "sell." Finch could easily be a big *F* on a one-inch ruler. Mr. Culpepper could be gulping pepper; and Mr. Ramsey, with a big old ram, could be riding on a sightseeing bus "to see what he could see." The seemingly difficult names are the easiest ones to recall. Just picture Mr. Yankowski as a man yanking a cow on skis.

Yankowski

Selman is a name I missed once. I'll never forget it. I failed to associate the name with something definite and it did embarrass me. It could have been associated with the famous Cardinal Spellman or I could have Mr. Selman being sold in an ancient slave market. There are many ways to reach a perfect or near-perfect picturization of anyone you meet.

Desire — Repetition — Visualization — Association — these are the keys to name retention.

Remember: Desire — Repetition — Visualization — Association — these are the keys to success.

PHOTOGRAPHS

....

Here is Mr. Martin. He is a smart man—smart in many ways. "Smart in," Martin. He has a small mouth. A marten is a small animal and has a small mouth, too.

Let me introduce Mr. Fleming. He has heavy eyebrows. Picture these notable eyebrows on fire. Mr. Fleming's eyebrows will be flaming.

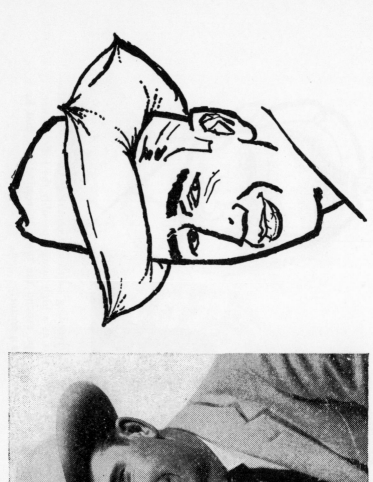

Presenting Mr. Cushman. He is wearing a hat as large as a cushion. More important, his lips are prominent and look as soft as a cushion. If you think of cushion you'll remember Cushman.

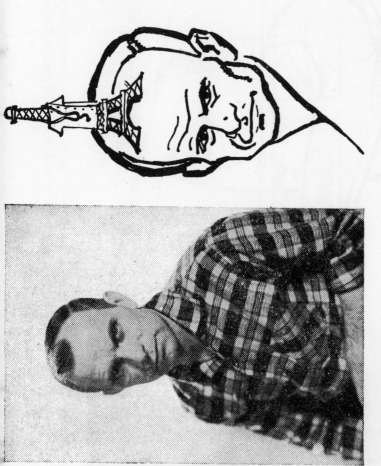

Take a look at Dr. Hightower. His receding hairline accentuates the "tower" of hair left at the center, so picture this as a high tower—possibly the Eiffel Tower. Put a white jacket and a stethoscope around the tower to remind you that he is a doctor.

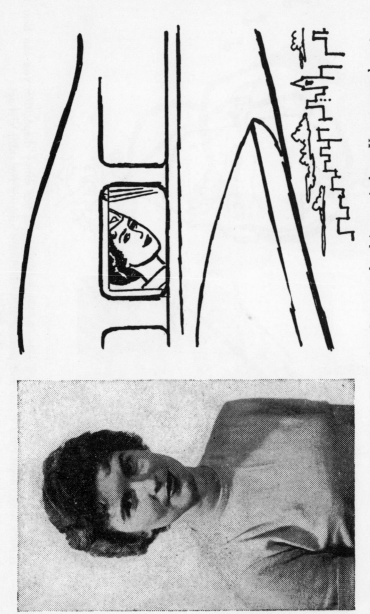

This pretty miss is Miss Haverland. Picture her flying overhead in an airplane. You can see her at the window. She is so pretty that you'd like her to be near you. You shout up to the pilot. "Have her land." And now you won't forget the name Haverland.

This smiling young lady is Miss Robinson. There's a robin in her name and in her sunny disposition you can hear the robin's song. Repeat the name and picture Miss Robinson singing the robin's song.

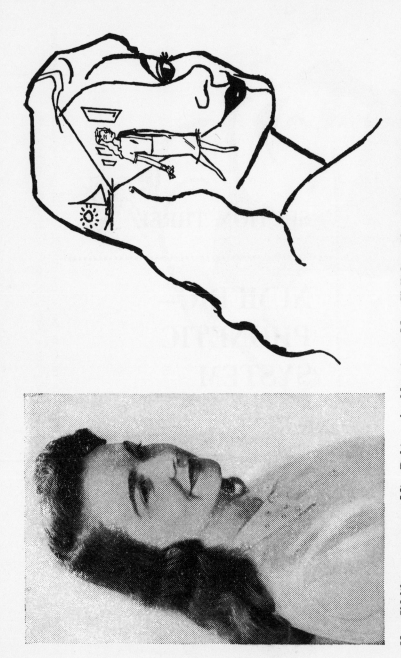

Now I'd like you to meet Miss Robinson's older sister, Mrs. Halliday. She is so nice that if she were my secretary she would only have to work half a day. I'd like to see her walking toward me down the hall all day, or picture her on a holiday.

SECTION THREE

NUMERIC—
PHONETIC
SYSTEM

ALPHABETICAL AND
NUMERICAL AIDS

THE FIRST SECTION of this book presented a simplified method for memorization. We shall now deal with figures and with a permanent filing system.

Figures, if pictured as articles in a scene of life, can be more easily retained. If you will study the accompanying chart, you will find that the consonants represent figures. The vowels are always silent so far as figures are concerned. The code itself is based on phonetic spelling and pronunciation. In order to become adept at memorizing numerals, you should study this table.

The letters *t* and *d*, which have almost the same sound, were chosen to represent the figure 1 because they have only one downward stroke, and with either a crossbar or a loop can be converted to the figure 1. The letter *n* equals number 2, because of its two downward strokes, and the letter *m* equals number 3, because its three downward strokes touch a line at three places. The letter *r* equals number 4, because *r* is the fourth letter in the word *four* and the dominant sound. Number five is represented by capital letter *L*, which is the Roman numeral for 50 and 5 is the initial unit of this number. A *J* turned backwards looks like the number 6 and therefore represents it; the sounds of *j*, soft *g* or *ch*, and *sh* equal six also. The number 7 is represented by the letter *k*, since there are seven days in the weeK, and this can be pictured with the *K outstanding. F* or *V* equals 8. Picture a figure skater making a Figure 8 on the ice and you have the clue to this number. Number 9 is represented by the letter *P*, which looks like a 9 backwards; *B*, which sounds so much like *P* also equals 9. For number 0 you think of zero, so *z* equals 0; the *s* and soft *c* also equal 0.

Now that you have studied this table, it would be well for you to practice a few words. The word *at*, for instance, equals the figure 1. The word *hat* equals the figure 1. The word *hate* equals the figure 1.

1= t or d   One downward stroke; add a crossbar or a loop and you have *t* or *d*.

2= n   Two downward strokes covered by a loop.

3= m   Three downward strokes covered by connecting loops.

4= r   The fourth letter of the word *four* is r, and this is also the dominant sound.

5= L   L is the Roman numeral for number 50 and 5 is the first unit of this number.

6= J   6 looks like a J backwards. The sounds "ch," "sh," and "soft g" are like the sound of J, and so 6 can represent these too.

7= K   There are 7 days in the *weeK*. The sounds of the "hard g," "hard ch" and "ng" can also be shown by the number 7.

8= F or V   Picture in your magic eye a Figure Skater gliding across the ice and making a Figure 8 and you'll always remember this. V is said the same way as F by the mouth, only the voice is added.

9= P or B   9 looks like a P backwards, or a B without the lower loop backwards.

0= Z   Z as in zero, of course, because zero is 0. 0 can also stand for S and C, because the *SCore* at the start of every game is 0-0.

In or *an* equals the figure 2.
Home equals the figure 3.
Oar equals the figure 4.
Hill is the figure 5.
Age, shoe or *itch* equals the figure 6.
Cow or *ache* equals the figure 7.
Egg also equals 7.
Hive or *hoof* equals 8.
Hub equals 9.
Boy is also 9.
And *zoo* equals zero.

These are examples of how the phonetic sounds fit into the numeric system. In order to get a double number, 17 for instance, *d* would equal 1 and *g* equal 7. The word *dog* would therefore be 17. For the figure 99, the word would be *pipe* or *baby* or *pope* or *hubbub*.

When you have three numbers, you want a word like *church*, which would be 646; *gourd*, which would be 741; or *chained*, which would be 621. For a complete vocabulary, I suggest the following code words and the numbers that should represent them. You may vary these in order to fit them into your own "magic eye." They may be used indefinitely as a permanent filing system. They represent all numbers between 1 and 100. After you have learned these completely and thoroughly, you will be able to visualize immediately the number tied in with the object. If you wanted to do the magazine trick, for example, you could take Page 1 and put it with the first item, Page 2 with the second item, and so on.

Code Words and Numbers

1	hat	26	hinge
2	hen	27	ink
3	home	28	knife
4	oar	29	knob
5	hill	30	mice
6	hash	31	mud
7	cow	32	moon
8	hive	33	mummy
9	ape	34	mayor
10	dice	35	mule
11	tide	36	match
12	tin	37	muck
13	team	38	muff
14	tire	39	mop
15	till	40	rose
16	dish	41	rat
17	dog	42	rain
18	dove	43	ram
19	tub	44	roar
20	nose	45	rail
21	nod	46	roach
22	nun	47	rake
23	gnome	48	roof
24	snare	49	rope
25	nail	50	lace

51	light	76	cage
52	lion	77	cake
53	lamb	78	cuff
54	lawyer	79	cap
55	lily	80	vise
56	latch	81	feet
57	lake	82	fan
58	loaf	83	foam
59	lap	84	fire
60	cheese	85	file
61	sheet	86	fish
62	chain	87	fig
63	jam	88	fife
64	chair	89	fob
65	jail	90	bus
66	judge	91	boat
67	check	92	pin
68	chief	93	bomb
69	chop	94	bear
70	kiss	95	bell
71	kite	96	bush
72	can	97	bag
73	comb	98	beef
74	car	99	baby
75	coal	100	daisies

These should be practiced a great deal. If you will give yourself some exercises, such as writing down miscellaneous items then quickly filling in the code words that represent them, you will find that you will become very familiar with them in a short time. You may group two numbers by the following method. Suppose the number is 3255. You can picture a moon with a lily growing out of it. The 32 represents the moon and the 55 the lily. Number 1941 could be visualized as a tub (#19) with a rat (#41) running around it. You can make up additional words to supplement these if you desire, but learn these and use them as your permanent filing device.

To remember telephone numbers, you can memorize the exchange through the same system as that for memorizing a person's name. It may be visualized and repeated and pictured into a story that ties in with the numbers that you take out of this numeric–phonetic system.

CONCLUSION

Now that you have finished studying this book, sit back a moment and think how far you've come.

Having mastered the principles of the Auto-Magic* Memory Method and the one hundred numeric–phonetic code words in Section Three, you have at your fingertips a powerful tool—the ability to call to mind every fact, face and figure you will ever need to know.

Your training isn't finished, however, To be expert with the Auto-Magic* method, you must practice it. Start using it now in every memory task you face.

The Auto-Magic* method will never fail you. If you should ever encounter a situation in which the Auto-Magic* method doesn't provide you immediately with the stored-away knowledge you wish to use, don't be alarmed. RELAX, and you will find that in almost no time the information will flash to mind, because relaxation makes the mind receptive to recall.